THE BEST OF
SCOTTISH COOKING
in colour

DIONE PATTULLO

JOHNSTON & BACON
EDINBURGH and LONDON

A JOHNSTON & BACON book published by
Cassell & Collier Macmillan Publishers Ltd.
35 Red Lion Square, London WC1R 4SG
and Tanfield House, Tanfield Lane, Edinburgh EH3
5LL
and at Sydney, Auckland, Toronto, Johannesburg
an affiliate of
Macmillan Publishing Co.
New York

First Published in this Edition 1979

ISBN 0 7179 4255 4
Typeset by Inforum Ltd., Portsmouth
Printed in Great Britain, by Morrison & Gibb, London
and Edinburgh

THE BEST OF
SCOTTISH COOKING
in colour

Contents

Acknowledgements

Colour photographs by A L Hunter Photography, Edinburgh
Drawings by Gabrielle Stoddart

The author would also like to thank the following for their assistance:

The Kitchen Range, William Street, Edinburgh, for the loan of many accessories used in the photographs

George Campbell & Sons, Stafford Street, Edinburgh, for the loan of the grouse

John Dickson & Son Ltd., Frederick Street, Edinburgh, for the loan of the gun

The Scottish Milk Marketing Board for the loan of cheeses

Miss Phillipa Ware, for her assistance in the preparation of food for photography

Mrs Marion Brown and Mrs Jenny Carter for the loan of accessories

Introduction

The traditional dishes of any country derive from the foods locally available. And Scotland is geographically perfect for the production of first class foods. The varied coastline produces not only excellent firm-fleshed white fish but an abundance of fine flavoured shellfish. Lobsters and crab, and scampi from the north have no equal. Inland are lush pastures which fatten the fine beef cattle, and lambs are reared in the foothills.

Further up on the hills graze deer, and a wide variety of gamebirds are found — red grouse and partridge, and in the lower woods pheasant, snipe and woodcock. Hares and rabbits were always plentiful, and figured largely in traditional cooking as a cheap and easily available meat.

Central Scotland produces some of the best raspberries in the world. Other soft fruits also do well, and in the wild are delicious cranberries and blueberries. Oatmeal is used widely, not only in the well-known bowl of porridge, but in haggis, in white puddings, oatcakes and oatmeal fritters, a personal favourite.

The Viking invaders showed us the arts of smoking and curing, and the Auld Alliance with France saw the introduction of wines and brandies in cooking. As the traffic in sugar and spices with the Indies grew, so did the baker's repertoire, and today Scotland is justly renowned for her fine range of scones, cakes and shortbreads.

In *The Best of Scottish Cooking* I give you some of these traditional recipes, and some you

7

may not have tried before. Discover for yourself that there is more to Scottish cooking than porridge!

Measures

Throughout the book, pounds and ounces (Imperial) measures have been used. If you wish to weigh your ingredients in kilos and grammes, a conversion ratio of 25 grammes to one ounce will give satisfactory results for most recipes.

In some recipes, especially in the Baking section, this ratio was not always suitable, and for this reason separate conversions have been given for a number of recipes.

Cup measures are based on a standard 6 fluid ounce measure, and spoons are measured level British standard spoons.

American measures are very slight compared to British standard measures, but all the recipes in this book are fairly flexible, and a generous American measure should compare roughly with a level British measure.

Quantities

Most recipes in this book are designed to feed 4-6 persons. This depends on the appetite of those fed, or the pocket of the cook.

Approximate Oven Temperatures

Follow guidance given in individual recipes.

Cool	225°F	110°C	Gas ¼
Slow	300°F	150°C	Gas 2
Moderately Slow	325°F	160°C	Gas 3
Moderate	350°F	180°C	Gas 4
Moderately Hot	375°F	190°C	Gas 5
Hot	400°F	200°C	Gas 6
Very Hot	425°F	220°C	Gas 7

Scotch Broth

¼-½ *lb neck of mutton*
1 pint cold water
½ oz barley
pepper and salt
¼ pint diced turnip and carrot
½ leek, sliced
1 carrot, grated
½ teaspoon minced parsley

Wipe the meat. Put into a pan with enough cold water to cover. Add the salt and the well-washed barley. Bring the water to boiling point and skim. Add pepper, diced vegetables, leek. Simmer for 1½ hours. Half an hour before serving add the grated carrot. When ready lift out the meat and cut into dice and return the flesh to the pan. Add the parsley and reboil for a moment before serving.

Cock-a-leekie Soup

1 boiling fowl
salt and pepper
bay, and sweet herbs (thyme, marjoram, etc)
8-10 leeks
8 prunes soaked in water

Put the boiling fowl on to simmer in as much water as it needs to cover well. Skim, and then add the salt, pepper and herbs. Clean the leeks and cut into 1-inch pieces. Wash again to get rid of any remaining grit, and half way through the cooking of the fowl, add them to the pot. When the fowl is tender, remove it to a serving dish for use later. Add the prunes to the soup remaining, and cook for a further 30 minutes. Sprinkle with chopped parsley before serving.

Partan Bree

6 oz rice
1 pint milk
1 crab
1½ pints white stock
anchovy essence
pepper and salt
mace
¾ pint cream

Boil the rice in the milk until soft. Take the meat out of the crab and set aside the claw meat. Sieve the rice, milk and soft crab meat. Stir in stock, anchovy essence and seasoning. Salt may not be needed if the essence is very strong. Reheat gently and add a pinch of mace and the cream and garnish with the flaked claw meat and cayenne.

Oatmeal Soup

1 onion
1 carrot
1 small white turnip
1 leek
2 oz dripping
1 oz oatmeal
1 pint stock
salt and pepper
¾ pint milk
parsley to garnish

Peel and dice the vegetables finely. Melt the dripping in the pan and sweat the vegetables in this for 10 minutes with the lid on. Add the oatmeal and fry for a few minutes. Add the stock and cook for 45 minutes. Add seasoning and milk. Reheat and serve, garnished with parsley.

Hare Soup

1 hare, skinned and jointed
1 tablespoon vinegar
4 oz streaky bacon
1 onion
1 stick celery
piece carrot
piece turnip
fresh herbs
potato flour
1 tablespoon redcurrant jelly
salt and pepper
1 gill ruby port

Take the hare, slit its throat carefully and save the blood. Add the vinegar to prevent it clotting. Brown the bacon and the onion together in a thick-bottomed pan. Do not let them burn. Add the hare and enough water to cover it well, and salt and pepper. Simmer for 2 hours. Add the rest of the vegetables and herbs. Top up with extra water if needed and simmer for a further 2 hours. Strain into a clean bowl. Shred the meat finely and return to the soup. Blend the potato flour with cold water to make a runny paste and stir into the soup. Bring to the boil and allow to thicken slightly. Add the blood and the jelly. Reheat without boiling or it will curdle. Finally, season, stir in the port and serve with meat balls.

Spring Vegetable Soup

½ bunch spring onions
1 small leek
2-3 small carrots
1 stick celery
1 small potato
2 pints of guinea fowl stock
parsley

Clean, peel and cut into small dice all the vegetables. Bring the stock to the boil and toss in the vegetables. Season and simmer for 30 minutes. When ready to serve add some minced parsley.

Lentil Soup

6 oz lentils
2 carrots
piece turnip
2 onions
2 sticks celery
3 oz fat bacon
ham bone, if available
2 pints stock
1 gill milk

Soak the lentils overnight in cold water, making sure they are properly washed and picked over. Clean and dice the vegetables. Cut the bacon into small pieces and fry gently in some extra fat until the fat is run. Add the lentils and sauté gently for a few minutes. Add the rest of the vegetables, stirring thoroughly to make sure the lentils do not stick. Add the bone, if available, and the stock. Simmer until the vegetables are soft, about 40 minutes. Put the soup through a blender or mouli and check the seasoning. Remember there will be some salt from the ham bone. Finally add a gill of milk and reheat. Serve with sippets, tiny triangles of toasted bread.

Nettle Soup

1½ lb young nettles
1 lb spinach
1 pint bone stock
salt and pepper
cooked sausages
2 tablespoons sour cream

Blanch nettles and mix with washed spinach. Bring to the boil with the stock and seasoning, and simmer for 30-40 minutes. Add more stock should it be needed. Sieve and return to pan. Add the sliced sausages and sour cream.
(N.B. Italian sausage is good with this.)

Cullen Skink

1 medium finnan haddock
1 chopped onion
1 pint milk
mashed potato as needed
½ oz butter
salt and pepper
mace
1-2 tablespoons cream
parsley

Skin the haddock. Place in a shallow pan, and add just enough hot water to cover. Bring slowly to the boil. Simmer until the haddock turns creamy. Take it out of the pan and remove the flesh from the bones. Flake the fish. Return the bones to the water in the pan and add the onion. Cover and simmer gently for 40 minutes. Strain this stock. Return to a clean pan and bring to the boil. In another pan bring the milk to the boil and add to the stock with the fish. Simmer gently for about 5 minutes. Stir in enough hot mashed potato to make a creamy consistency. Add butter bit by bit and salt, pepper and mace to taste. Stir in the cream and a heaped tablespoon of chopped parsley.

Opposite: Skirley, Scotch Broth and Cullen Skink

Game Soup

2 onions
2 carrots
2 sticks celery
1 tablespoon lard
game carcases
peppercorns
salt
potato flour
madeira

Chop the onions, peel and slice the carrots and wash and slice the celery. Brown the onions in the lard, making sure they do not burn. Add the other vegetables, the broken carcases of the birds and the seasoning. Add sufficient water to cover well and bring to the boil. Simmer for 2 hours. Strain through a sieve and put into a fresh pan. Mix 2 or 3 teaspoons of potato flour with some cold water to a runny consistency. Stir into the warm stock and bring to the boil to thicken. Correct the seasoning if necessary and add, if available, the meat from the drumsticks of the smaller birds which are not readily edible with a knife and fork. Cut this meat into small dice. Stir in the madeira. Serve in hot bowls with chopped parsley.

Opposite: Arbroath Smokies

Tattie Drottle

2 carrots
1 small piece turnip
2 large leeks
2 lb potatoes
2 pints white stock
2 pints milk
pepper and salt

Prepare and dice the vegetables and potatoes, cutting the leeks into small pieces. Boil vegetables in stock until cooked. Add milk and season. Bring back to the boil and serve with oatcakes.

Onion Soup

4 large onions
1½ pints milk
salt and pepper
parsley or chervil

Peel and chop the onions. Boil in some water for 5 minutes and drain. Put the onions back in the rinsed pan with the milk and the seasoning. Cook until tender and serve with a good sprinkling of parsley or chervil.

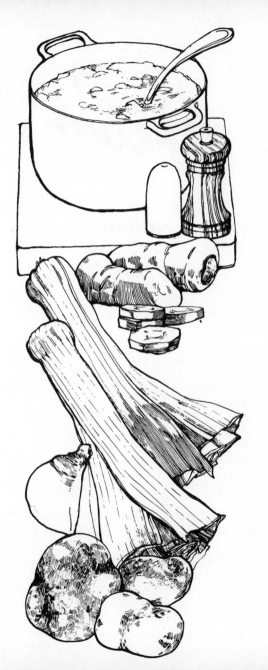

Poached Salmon

>1 salmon
>lemons
>parsley
>melted butter

Court bouillon

>sole bones
>peppercorns
>bay leaf
>blade mace
>lemon rind
>water
>salt

Make the court bouillon by boiling all the ingredients under that heading in a large pan for not more than 20 minutes. Strain into a clean fish kettle. Put the fish onto the straining plate and lower into the stock. Bring to the boil and simmer gently for 10 minutes per pound weight of fish.

Drain carefully and dish onto a warmed ashet. Garnish with lily-cut lemons and parsley. Serve with melted butter and new potatoes.

If served cold, allow to cool in the fish liquid. When cold, drain and skin carefully. Place on a large plate or fish board and garnish with butterfly lemon slices, cucumber and half a stuffed olive in the eye socket. Serve with a good home-made mayonnaise and cucumber salad.

Potted Lobster

2-3 lb hen lobster
salt
pepper
cayenne
mace
lemon juice
butter to cover

Boil the lobster for 12-15 minutes. Crack the shell and discard the stomach and black intestinal vein. Take out the meat keeping it as whole as possible. Line a small loaf tin with non-stick paper. Slice the tail meat of the lobster and arrange attractively in the bottom of the tin, alternating with bits of the coral. Over this arrange the lesser bits of meat. Sprinkle each layer lightly with the seasonings and lemon juice. When all the meat is used, lightly press it down and pour over enough melted butter to cover. Bake in a tin of water for 30 minutes at 300°F (Gas 2). Cool and chill. Dip the tin in hot water and turn out. Slice with a sharp knife.

Kipper Stuffed Eggs

1 medium kipper
6 hard boiled eggs
1-2 tablespoons cream
salt and pepper
mace
cream

Place the kipper in a non-metal container and add half a gill of water. Cover and bake for about 25 minutes. Cool and then carefully remove the skin and bones. Mash the flesh well with a fork. Halve the eggs longways, add the yolks to the kipper and mash them together. Add enough cream to make into a soft stuffing. Season with pepper and mace and check before adding salt to the already salty kipper mix. Heap the filling up roughly in the egg whites and garnish with a small sprig of fennel.

Salmon Mousse

1 tablespoon gelatine
2 tablespoons cold water
2 eggs
pepper to taste
1 teaspoon mustard
1 teaspoon salt
½ tablespoon plain flour
1½ tablespoons sugar
¾ cup milk
¼ cup white wine vinegar

1½ tablespoons melted butter
1 tin salmon
½ cup double cream

Soften gelatine in the water. Put the eggs, seasoning, flour and sugar in the top of a double boiler, and whisk over boiling water until smooth. Add milk and vinegar and continue whisking until mix thickens. Add butter and melted gelatine. Stir. Add the flaked salmon and chill, stirring from time to time. When slightly thickened fold in the half-whipped cream and turn into a mould.

Baked Sea Trout

1 sea trout, 2-3 lb
fresh tarragon
2 oz butter
salt and pepper
lemon to garnish

Wash the fish inside and out and dry with paper towels. Put a small spray of tarragon in the fish and spread the butter on the outside. Lay on a sheet of foil and sprinkle with salt and pepper. Wrap loosely in the foil and put in a dish. Bake in a moderate oven (350°F, Gas 4) for about 45 minutes or until the fish lifts easily from the backbone. Put on a serving dish and garnish with lemon wedges. Serve with melted butter in a sauce boat.

Poached Trout with Pink Mayonnaise

6 whole trout, cleaned
white wine court bouillon (see page 20)
cucumber, lemon and hard-boiled egg for garnish

Place the fish on a grid and drop into the boiling court bouillon. Simmer for 10 minutes. Drain. Arrange on a platter. Chill. Take a strip of skin off the middles, making a diagonal pattern across. Leave the heads and tails intact. Garnish with pieces of unpeeled cucumber at the head, and a slice of lemon and sliced hard-boiled egg. Top with fresh tarragon or sliced stuffed olive.

Transfer fish carefully onto a bed of mayonnaise (see below).

Pink Mayonnaise

1 cup mayonnaise, blended into 1/3 cup tomato purée, juice of a lemon, teaspoon grated lemon rind, salt and pepper to taste.

Herring Pie

6 herring
6 potatoes
1 apple
2 shallots
salt and pepper

Clean and bone the herring. Soak in salted water for ½ hour. Parboil the potatoes. Core and chop the apple and peel and chop the shallots. Butter a baking dish and fill with alternate layers of sliced potato, herring fillets and shallot mix. Season each layer. Top with a final layer of potatoes and add a cup of water. Cover and bake in a moderate oven (350°F, Gas 4) for 45 minutes.

Herring in Sour Cream

4 fresh herring
½ onion, finely chopped
4 tablespoons double cream
salt and freshly ground black pepper
1 tablespoon pickling spice
dry cider or white wine
¼ pint sour cream
cucumber

Wash and scale the herring. Sprinkle with a little of the chopped onion, salt and pepper and pour on the double cream. Roll up the herring from head to tail. Sprinkle the rest of the chopped onion on the bottom of a shallow heatproof dish. Add the pickling spice and arrange the fish on this layer. Pour in wine or cider to just cover. Bake in a moderate oven (375°F, Gas 5) until fish flakes easily. Cool and remove the fish. Strain the cooking liquid and blend with the sour cream. Season with salt and freshly ground black pepper. Arrange the fish on a serving dish and pour over the sour cream sauce. Garnish with thinly-sliced unpeeled cucumber.

Loch Leven Trout

  3 medium brown or rainbow trout
  seasoned flour
  1½ oz butter
  2 oz flaked browned almonds
  3 tablespoons whisky
  lemon

Toss the cleaned fish in seasoned flour. Melt the butter and when it is frothing put in the fish. Cook for 5 minutes on each side. Add the almonds and toss lightly until hot. Pour in the whisky and flame, shaking the pan until the flame dies. Add a squeeze of lemon juice to taste and serve very hot with lemon wedges. *Serves 3.*

Smoked Salmon Pâté

  4 oz smoked salmon scraps
  1 oz butter
  2 tablespoons cream
  black pepper
  mace
  lemon juice

Put all the ingredients into a blender or use a pestle and mortar. When the mixture is quite smooth, check for seasoning, and pack into very small containers. Use as soon as possible as an hors d'oeuvre or on toasted canapés. Top with a pinch of cayenne.

Arbroath Smokies

4 whole smoked haddock
¾ pint milk
salt and pepper
butter

Split the pairs of Arbroath smokies and lay them in a shallow dish. Pour on the milk and a little salt and pepper. Dot with butter and cover with foil or with a piece of greaseproof paper to prevent drying out. Cook in a moderate oven (350°F, Gas 4) for 25-30 minutes. Serve hot.

Kippers

While herring are scarce and kippers cost almost as much as smoked salmon, it is a pity not to cook them the best possible way. There are two ways I have found satisfactory:

1) Put the headed and tailed kippers into a china, pottery or pyrex glass container. (Metal retains the smell and can affect other dishes.) Put on each a small dab of butter and add one or two tablespoons of water. Cover with a lid or tinfoil, and bake in a moderate oven for 15 to 20 minutes.
2) Head and tail the kippers. Put into a skillet with a quarter inch of water. Cover with the lid and allow to simmer very gently for 8 to 10 minutes. Drain and serve.

Kipper Pâté 1

2 kippers
butter
salt and black pepper
lemon juice

Bake the fish in a non-metal container with a small quantity of water. When cooked, cool and carefully remove the skin and bones. Weigh the flesh and add an equal quantity of butter. Put through a mouli or blender and season with fresh black pepper, lemon juice to taste and salt if needed. Pack into ramekin dishes and run butter over the top to keep.

Kipper Pâté 2

6-8 oz kipper fillets
3-4 oz butter
2-3 tablespoons double cream
paprika
ground black pepper
mace

Blanch kippers and drain well. Remove flesh and put in blender with the softened butter. Add cream and season to taste. Chill before use, or pipe onto water biscuits or fingers of toast. Decorate with sieved yolk and white of egg, finely chopped parsley, gherkin fans, walnuts, or olives, etc.

Potted Herring

12 herring
salt and pepper
½ cup vinegar
¾ cup water

Roll up the herring from head to tail. Lay them close to each other in a shallow baking dish. Sprinkle with salt and pepper and add the liquids. Cover with foil and bake in a moderate oven (350°F, Gas 4) for ½ hour. Cool and serve cold with a salad, preferably new potato salad.

Scampi Flamed in Whisky

2 oz butter
12 oz scampi
salt and fresh black pepper
2 tablespoons whisky
watercress
cooked rice in a ring (see page 46)

Melt the butter in a skillet and when it is frothing add the scampi. Season and toss over a moderate heat for 3-4 minutes. Add the whisky and set it alight at once. Shake the pan until the flame dies. Pour into the centre of a hot rice ring. Garnish with watercress.

Game

Venison Chops

Season cutlets with salt and pepper. Grill them slowly, and serve with venison sauce (see below) or with redcurrant jelly.

Venison Sauce

> *1 oz currants*
> *3 tablespoons grated breadcrumbs*
> *½ oz butter*
> *4 cloves*
> *glass of port wine*

Boil the currants in water for a few minutes. Add the rest of the ingredients and stir until boiling. Serve hot with roast venison.

Stuffed Venison Rolls

> *1 lb venison, sliced thinly*
> *butter to fry*

1 carrot, chopped
1 onion, chopped
1 stick celery, sliced
salt and pepper
fresh thyme

Marinade

1 onion, chopped
½ teaspoon fresh thyme
2 bay leaves
salt and black pepper
8-10 juniper berries, lightly crushed
½ bottle red wine

Stuffing

1 onion, chopped
2-3 rashers streaky bacon, snipped small
4 oz butter

Soak the venison in the marinade for 24 hours. Strain off the marinade, reserving it. To make the stuffing, sauté the onion with the bacon in the butter. Add 3 tablespoons of the marinade, and fry for a moment. Add another 2 tablespoons of the marinade. Divide the stuffing between the slices of meat, and wrap up with a slice of bacon on the outside. Secure with a roulade needle, or tie with thread. Fry in a casserole in the butter, adding the carrot, onion and celery. Add the strained marinade and stock just to cover. Add seasoning and fresh thyme. Casserole for 1½ hours at 350°F, Gas 4.

To make without the stuffing, just drain the meat dry after marinating, and brown it. Re-add the marinade and season with thyme. Casserole for 1½ hours, in a moderate oven (350°F, Gas 4).

Roast Pheasant with 'Bols'

1 or more young pheasants
salt and pepper
streaky bacon
butter
6 tablespoons Bols Very Old Genever
thick cream
tinned apricots
apricot brandy
toasted chopped almonds

Hold the pheasant quickly under boiling water, rub with salt and pepper and then roll it in thin slices of fat bacon. Hold these in place with a piece of thread or a skewer. Cook the pheasant with a little butter in a pan with a lid, either on top of the stove or in the oven, for 40-45 minutes, or until the bird is cooked. Remove the pheasant from the pan and flame with 6 spoons of Bols Very Old Genever. To facilitate the flaming, the spoon should first be thoroughly warmed. Cut into portions, arrange these in a shallow dish and keep hot. Heat up the cooking liquid and then slowly add the desired amount of scalded cream, a little at a time, while stirring. In this way the gravy should not curdle. Add salt and pepper to taste. Meanwhile heat the apricots in their juice.

Continued on page 33

Pour off the juice and sprinkle the fruit with a little apricot brandy. Carefully pour the cream sauce over the pheasant, arrange the apricots round it on the dish, and sprinkle them with a few toasted chopped almonds.

Previous page: Jellied Meat Mould (front) Rabbit Brawn, and on the board, Bacon Loaf (left) and Meat Roll.
Opposite: Forfar Bridies.

Venison Hash

bone and trimmings of cold roast venison
peppercorns
salt
flour to thicken
knob of butter
glass of port
1 tablespoon mushroom ketchup
1 tablespoon redcurrant jelly
slices of venison

Boil the bone and trimmings with water, pepper-corns and salt. Strain and thicken with flour and butter. Add port, ketchup and jelly. Heat and add slices of venison. Reheat thoroughly. Serve with sippets of toast.

Jugged Hare

1 hare and its blood
2 oz butter
2 oz fat bacon, chopped
1 clove garlic
2 bay leaves
2 cloves
1 small stick of cinnamon
1 oz flour
1 pint game stock
1 tablespoon redcurrant jelly
1 gill port
1 tablespoon Harvey's sauce
salt and pepper

Set aside the blood. Joint the hare and brown in the melted butter in which the chopped bacon has been sautéd. Put into a casserole. Tie the flavourings in butter muslin and add to the casserole with salt and stock. Cover and put in a pan adding hot water to just cover. Cook on the stove, covered, for 2½-3 hours. Dish the hare and keep hot. Mix the flour and some stock. Add the jelly to the thickened stock and cook for 4-5 minutes. Mix strained blood with port and add to the sauce. Season. Stir until it thickens but do not boil. Strain the sauce over the hare, and garnish with forcemeat balls.

Venison Soup

1 lb shank veal
2 lb breast of venison
4 oz lean ham
2 onions
1 teaspoon white peppercorns
salt
4 pints water
1 oz butter kneaded together with 1 oz flour
1 glass madeira

Simmer the meats in the water with the seasoning and onions for several hours. Remove the bone and put the soup through the liquidiser. Add the butter and flour mix and bring to the boil stirring all the time. Boil for 3-5 minutes and finally add a good glass of madeira. Simmer for a few more minutes and serve hot with parsley.

Salmis of Game

lightly-roasted pigeon or pheasant
button mushrooms
½ pint Espagnole sauce
½ gill port
1 dessertspoon redcurrant jelly
fleurons of pastry
cherries

Divide the lightly-roasted or cold cooked game into neat pieces for serving. Remove the skin and arrange in a casserole or ovenproof dish with the mushrooms. Heat the sauce and add the port and the redcurrant jelly. Pour over the meat, cover, and simmer gently until tender. Season to taste. Garnish with fleurons of pastry and a few cherries.

Stuffed Quails and Rice

1 oz lean sweet bacon
6 oz veal
2 oz fresh white breadcrumbs
salt and pepper
1 tablespoon brandy
little egg to bind
6 boned quails
knuckle of veal
8 oz rice
1 oz toasted, flaked almonds
2 oz raisins
watercress

Mince bacon and veal twice. Pound in pestle and mortar with the breadcrumbs and seasoning, including the brandy, until very fine. Add the egg to make a moist stuffing mix. Divide into six and stuff each quail with one portion. Wrap each individual bird in a well-buttered square of greaseproof paper, put in a buttered ovenproof casserole, packing tightly against each other. Cover with lid and cook in hot oven (400°F, Gas 6) for 18 minutes. Remove paper and glaze with a veal glaze made from veal knuckle. Cook the rice in salted water for 15 minutes. Drain well and dry. Toss in the toasted almonds and raisins. Pile the rice mixture in the middle of a dish and arrange the quails around it. Garnish with watercress and serve very hot.

Venison Pasty

2 lb neck or breast venison
sweet herbs (thyme, parsley, marjoram etc)
pepper and salt
juice of ½ lemon
grated nutmeg
½ lb puff pastry
½ pint rich gravy made with trimmings
glass port

Slice the meat thinly and put with sweet herbs, seasoning, lemon and nutmeg. Sauté lightly in butter and put into a pie dish lined with some of the pastry. Add the gravy and port, and cover with the rest of the pastry. Bake for 2 hours in a moderate oven. Some extra gravy may be added if it has dried out.

Grouse Pudding

1 old grouse
½ lb stewing meat
1 oz flour
12 oz suet crust pastry (see below)
2 oz streaky bacon
1 chopped onion
pinch thyme
small bay leaf
½ pint stock and red wine mixed

Cut the bird and meat into small pieces and dip in seasoned flour. Line a greased pudding bowl with 2/3 of the crust and add the meats, onions and herbs in layers. Pour over the stock and wine mix. Cover the top with the rest of the pastry. Make a hole in the lid, cover with a greased paper and put to steam for 3 hours.

Suet pastry

8 oz (200 grammes) plain flour
½ teaspoon salt
1 teaspoon baking powder
4 oz (100 grammes) chopped suet
cold water

Sift the flour, salt and baking powder into a bowl. Add the chopped or shredded suet, and mix in. Add cold water gradually to form a fairly soft dough. Turn onto a well-floured board for rolling out.

Quails in Champagne

6 quails
seasoning
1 gill champagne
1 split veal knuckle
watercress

Butter six squares of greaseproof paper large enough to wrap round the birds. Add the seasoning to the birds and wrap well. Put in a casserole and cook with a lid on in a hot oven (400°F, Gas 6) for 18 minutes. After 10 minutes unwrap the birds and pour in the champagne. Baste well. Have some veal stock made with the veal knuckle and use this to make a glaze for the birds using the juices and champagne in the casserole. Arrange the birds in a dish, and garnish with the watercress. Serve very hot.

Pheasant with Chestnuts in Red Wine

1 pheasant
1 oz butter
1 tablespoon olive oil
½ lb chestnuts (weighed when peeled and skinned)
½ lb button onions
about ¾ oz flour
¾-1 pint chicken or veal stock
grated rind and juice of ½ an orange
1 dessertspoon redcurrant jelly
1 good glass Burgundy or Beaujolais
bouquet garni, including parsley stalks, bay leaf, celery seeds and thyme
salt and pepper
parsley

Brown the pheasant slowly all over in the hot oil and butter. Place in casserole. Sauté the chestnuts and onions briskly until they begin to turn colour, shaking the pan frequently. Remove from the pan and place round pheasant. Add enough flour to take up the remaining fat. Cook this roux thoroughly. Blend the remaining ingredients, except the parsley, and bring to the boil. Pour over the pheasant and cover tightly. Cook in a slow to moderate oven (325°F-350°F, Gas 3-4) for 1½-2 hours. Remove the bouquet garni, skim the liquid and reduce if necessary. Adjust seasoning. Dust with chopped parsley and serve.

Game Pâté en Terrine

6-8 rashers streaky bacon
½-¾ of a young rabbit
3-4 oz liver
3-4 oz fresh pork
1 small onion, finely chopped
2 tablespoons finely chopped parsley
4 oz sausagemeat
1 oz breadcrumbs
milk
seasoning
pinch of nutmeg
1 small glass brandy
a little beaten egg
2 bay leaves
1-2 oz melted butter

Line the inside of a terrine with the rashers of bacon, reserving one or two for the top. Cut the rabbit into thin slices, carefully removing all bones. Finely chop the liver and pork. Mix the onion with the parsley. Add the liver, pork and sausagemeat and mix well. Soak the breadcrumbs in a little milk, squeeze them out until almost dry and beat them into the farce. Season well, add a pinch of nutmeg, the brandy and enough egg to make a slightly moist mixture. Spread a layer of this farce in the bottom of the lined terrine, and lay a few slices of rabbit on the top. Cover again with more farce and the rest of the rabbit. Finish with a layer of farce. It is important to fill the mould as the mixture shrinks in cooking. Place one or two rashers of bacon on the top, laying a bay leaf on these. Cover with greaseproof paper or aluminium foil and the lid. Stand the terrine in a baking dish with water half way up, and bake at 350°F (Gas 4) for 1¼ hours. Remove and half an hour later place a light weight (about 1 lb) on a saucer on the top of the terrine. Stand for 12 hours in a cool place. Remove the bay leaf and pour over a layer of melted butter. Replace a fresh bay leaf for decoration.

Game Terrine

1 pheasant
½ cup vermouth
½ cup whisky
peppercorns
¼ teaspoon garlic salt
8 oz minced bacon
3 or 4 pickled walnuts

Take the pheasant off the bone. Make a marinade with the vermouth, whisky, peppercorns and garlic salt. Marinate the bird for 24 hours. Line a loaf tin with some flattened streaky bacon and put in a layer of pheasant, then one of bacon. Lay the walnuts along the middle, cover with more of the minced bacon, and top with the pheasant. Cover with more bacon and a bay leaf. Bake at 350°F (Gas 4) for 1½-2 hours. Cool, turn out, chill and slice. Serve with hot-buttered toast.

Game Loaf

2 pigeons
marinade of vermouth, oil and bay
1 pheasant or 1 rabbit
6 oz minced bacon
mace
salt and pepper
few slices bacon

Bone the pigeons and marinate for 24 hours. Bone the pheasant or rabbit. Season the minced bacon with a pinch of mace, salt and freshly ground black pepper. Line a 2-lb loaf tin with bacon, and layer with the pheasant or rabbit first, the pigeon, the minced bacon and so on. Sprinkle liberally with the marinade between each layer. Top with streaky bacon and a bay leaf, and bake at 350°F, Gas 4 for 1½-2 hours. This keeps well in a freezer.

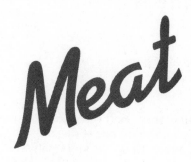

Rabbit Brawn

  1 rabbit
  salt and black pepper
  mace
  ½ lb ham
  1 hard boiled egg
  ½ oz gelatine
  1 pint good beef stock

Joint the rabbit and wipe with a paper towel.
Cover with water and add seasoning. Cook for
about 1½ hours, boiling very gently. Cut the ham
into ¼-inch cubes, and neatly slice the egg.
Arrange the egg round a basin and make a pattern
with the ham. Dissolve the gelatine in the stock.
Strain the rabbit and add the rabbit pieces to the
basin and just before the jelly sets pour it carefully over the meat. Allow to set. Turn out and
garnish with dill pickles and a sprig of fresh dill
if available.

Kilmany Kail

1 rabbit
4 oz pickled pork
2 heads kail

Cut the rabbit into small pieces and dice the pork. Take the tough stems out of the kail and wash it very thoroughly. Chop the kail finely. Put all the ingredients into a large pan and well cover with water or chicken stock. Add salt and pepper and simmer for 3 hours. Serve with fresh oatcakes and butter.

Skirley

3 handfuls oatmeal
½ lb suet
2 chopped onions
seasoning

Brown the meal in the oven on a baking sheet. Melt the suet and gently brown the onions. Add the oatmeal and seasoning. Fry very gently until well browned and cooked. Serve with mashed potatoes. This recipe can also be used as a stuffing for a fowl or for a duck.

Scots Collops

1 lb lean beef cut very thinly
1 oz butter
1 large onion, minced
1 oz flour
½ apple, minced
salt and pepper

Beat the meat until it is thin. Melt the butter and gently brown the onion, meat, flour and apple. Season with salt and pepper, add a little hot water to just cover and cover the pan. Simmer gently until tender, and serve with mashed potato.

Haggis Savoury Dish

1 small haggis
scrambled eggs
parsley

Prick the haggis with fork and wrap it up in a piece of tinfoil. Put onto a dish and bake in a moderate oven for about 1 hour. Have ready a hot serving dish and a pan of scrambled eggs. Spoon the haggis round the edge of the dish. Put the scrambled eggs in the middle and garnish with parsley.

Green Kail

2 heads kail
3 oz oatmeal
stock
salt and pepper
1 oz butter
1 gill cream

Wash and stem the kail. Boil for an hour in water.
Squeeze out the water and sieve the kail. Sprinkle
on the oatmeal. Return to the pan and add stock.
Boil for a few minutes and add the seasoning,
butter and warmed cream. Stir till it reheats and
serve with oatcakes.

Opposite: Pan Haggis (left) and Haggis
Next page: Cranberry Mousse (front) and Gaelic
Coffee Jelly

Baby's Leg

½ lb minced beef
½ lb minced ham
1 small onion, minced
3 oz porridge oats or oatmeal
1 egg
2 teaspoons Harvey's sauce or Worcester sauce
black pepper
¼ cup beef stock
browned breadcrumbs

Put beef, ham, onion, oats, egg, sauce, pepper and stock into a bowl. Mix well together using the hand, this being far easier than a fork. Well grease a 1 lb loaf tin, using beef dripping for the flavour, and pack mix into the tin. Stand in a baking tin with hot water half way up and put into a moderate oven 350°F (Gas 4). Cover with foil to prevent burning. After 2 hours remove from oven, take off the foil and fill to the brim with well-reduced beef stock made from bones or with the jelly from the bottom of the dripping. Cover with foil and weigh down. Cool. Roll in freshly browned breadcrumbs.

Previous page: Cranachan
Opposite: On the board, Oatcakes and Scones and on the girdle, Drop Scones (left) and Girdle Scones

Pan Haggis

1 lb liver
2 cups stock or water
3 onions
8 oz suet
2 cups oatmeal
salt and pepper

Boil the liver in the stock for 30-40 minutes. Reserve the liquid. Cool and grate the liver. Parboil the onions and chop them finely. Mince the suet if in the piece. Put the meal into a thick-based frying pan and hold over the heat stirring all the time until the oatmeal is browned. Add the liver, onion, suet and seasoning. Moisten with the liquid the liver was cooked in. Turn this mix into a greased pudding basin and cover. Steam for 2-3 hours and serve with mashed potato and turnip.

Bacon Loaf

1 lb minced bacon
1 lb minced pork
1 cup fresh breadcrumbs
1 egg
salt and pepper
1 dessertspoon brown sugar
1 dessertspoon ground cloves
½ cup milk
streaky bacon rashers

Mix the minced bacon and pork. Mix the rest of the ingredients, except rashers, and leave to soak for 5 minutes. Add the meat, and mix well. Line a 2-lb loaf tin with the rashers. Pack the meat mix in and bake in a slow oven (300°F, Gas 2) for 1½-2 hours. Turn out and serve hot with fresh tomato sauce or cold with a salad. *Serves 8-10.*

Clapshot

3 lb potatoes, peeled
1½ lb turnip, peeled and sliced
salt and pepper
2 oz butter

Soak the potatoes in a bowl of water. Boil the turnip in salted water for 15 minutes, then add the potatoes and boil for a further 20 minutes. Drain in a colander. Put back in the pan with the butter, and mash. Serve with haggis or meat such as corned beef.

Mince Collops

½ lb minced steak
1 teaspoon flour
1 gill stock, heated
pepper and salt
1 small onion
toasted or fried croûtons

Place the mince into a stewpan and brown it carefully, breaking up the lumps by beating well with a fork or wooden spoon. Sprinkle in the flour and mix thoroughly with the meat. Add the hot stock and a pinch of salt. Bring to the boil and season with pepper. Add the onion, skinned, but left whole. Simmer for about 1 hour stirring frequently. Remove the onion. Pile the mince on a hot ashet, and garnish with the croûtons.

Forfar Bridies

1 lb puff pastry
1 lb rump steak
2 finely chopped onions
2 oz chopped suet
1 beaten egg

Roll out the pastry and cut into 3 ovals. Beat the meat out thinly with a steak hammer and cut it into strips about 1 inch long. Should coarser beef be used, mince it before use. Season the meat and mix with the onion and the suet. Pile the meat mix onto the pastry and fold over. Seal the pastry with the egg and crimp the edges with finger and thumb. Brush the pastry with the rest of the egg. Place on a baking sheet and form small holes in each bridie to allow steam to escape in the cooking. Bake in a hot oven (450°F, Gas 7) for 20 minutes and then reduce the heat to 350°F (Gas 4) for a further hour to cook the meat. Serve hot.

Haggis

1 sheep's paunch
heart, lung and liver of sheep
salt
white and cayenne pepper
nutmeg
2 onions, chopped
6 oz toasted oatmeal
1 lb beef suet
¾ pint stock

Wash the paunch thoroughly. Turn it inside out. Boil the heart, liver and lung until tender. The windpipe must hang over the edge of the pan so that it drains into a bowl. Chop the meat very finely and grate the liver. Spread this over the table and add salt, pepper, nutmeg, onions, suet and oatmeal. Mix well with stock and fill into the paunch. Leave room for the oatmeal to swell in the cooking. Sew up, prick all over with a needle and put into boiling water for 3 hours. When reheating wrap in foil and bake in the oven for 2 hours, then if the bag bursts none of the filling will be lost.

Meat Roll

1 lb minced beef
6 oz minced ham
3 oz fresh white breadcrumbs
¼ pint milk
1 minced onion
1 egg
¼ teaspoon nutmeg
1 teaspoon fresh thyme
pepper and salt

Mix all the ingredients well in a large bowl.
Brush a meat roll jar with melted fat and push the
mix well into it. Cover with greaseproof paper
and tie down. Stand in a deep pan in boiling
water and allow it to simmer for 2 hours. Turn it
out once it is cold and roll it in browned breadcrumbs. Serve cold with salads.

Stewed Brisket

4-5 lb brisket
½ lb streaky bacon
4 onions
4 carrots
2 small white turnips
bay leaves, thyme
2 cloves
pinch allspice
salt and pepper
1 cup port wine
1 cup sherry

Put the brisket and bacon in a pan and add the peeled and sliced vegetables. Add the herbs, cloves, and allspice, and salt and pepper. Pour in the port and sherry and add sufficient water to cover the meat well. Set it to stew gently for 4-5 hours. Take out the beef, and strain off the stock. Skim the fat off as much as possible, and use kitchen paper towels to take off the rest. Boil some fresh vegetables in this stock and thicken with a little potato flour before pouring round the beef.

Jellied Meat Mould

2 lb shin of beef
1 nap bone
1 pig's foot
2 cloves
8 peppercorns
¼ teaspoon mace
salt for seasoning
water to well-cover

Put all the ingredients into a large strong pan and bring to the boil. A scum will rise which should be removed with a large spoon. Simmer very steadily for 5 hours. Remove meat and cut off any fat and gristle. Mince the meat and put into a fresh pan. Strain over the liquid in which it was cooked. Bring to the boil and boil for a couple of minutes. Pour into 2 or 3 wetted moulds and allow to set in a cool place. Keep in the moulds until needed and serve with some well-flavoured salads. *Serves 8*.

Gypsy Pie

1 rabbit
½ lb steak
¼ lb sausagemeat
salt and pepper
parsley, chopped finely
grated rind of ½ lemon
stock
1 lb puff pastry

Joint the rabbit and cut up the steak in fine pieces. Form the sausagemeat into small balls. Arrange in a pie dish. Season and add the parsley and the lemon rind. Add stock and cover the pie with the pastry. Cook slowly for 1½-2 hours.

Sweets

Blaeberries in Lemon Cream

2 eggs, separated
¼ cup sugar
2½ tablespoons lemon juice
1 teaspoon grated lemon rind
¼ cup double cream
fresh blaeberries

In a bowl beat yolks until they are thick and pale.
Beat in the sugar, lemon juice and rind. Cook in
the top of a double boiler until thick, stirring all
the time. Cool and fold in one of the egg whites,
stiffly beaten, the cream lightly beaten and the
berries. Pour into 2 long-stemmed glasses and
garnish with extra berries. Chill well before
serving. *Serves 2.*

Raspberry Almond Tart

1 lb fresh raspberries
sugar to sweeten
8 oz plain flour
pinch salt
1 teaspoon cinnamon
2½ oz ground unblanched almonds
4 oz butter
4 oz castor sugar
1 whole egg
1 egg yolk
grated rind of ½ lemon
redcurrant jelly

Bring the raspberries, sugared to taste, quickly to the boil and cook rapidly for 4-5 minutes to make a 'marmalade'. Turn onto a plate to cool. Sieve the flour, salt and cinnamon onto the table and form into a ring. Sprinkle with the almonds. Place the butter, sugar, egg and yolk, and lemon rind in the centre. Work these ingredients together and knead into a dough. Cover and leave in a cool place for ½-1 hour. Roll out the chilled dough to ¼-½-inch thickness. Line a 7-inch flan ring, trim and fill with the cold raspberry 'marmalade'. Roll out the trimmings thinly, cut into strips and make a lattice across the top. Bake at 375°F (Gas 5) for 25-30 minutes. Allow to cool slightly before removing the flan ring. Brush over with melted redcurrant jelly.

Scottish Crumble

1½ lb (700 grammes) rhubarb or cooking
apples
2 oz (30 grammes) flour
2 tablespoons porridge oats

2 oz (30 grammes) demerara sugar
4 oz (50 grammes) butter
2 oz (30 grammes) granulated sugar
2 teaspoons ground ginger
2-3 tablespoons water

Grease a pie dish and put in it the washed and
sliced fruit. Mix the flour, oats and demerara
sugar, and rub in the butter. Mix the granulated
sugar and ginger and sprinkle over the fruit. Add
the water. Spread the crumble mix over the fruit
and bake in a moderate oven (350°F, Gas 4) for 40-
45 minutes.

Caledonian Cream

    1 tablespoon marmalade
    2 fluid oz brandy
    2 oz castor sugar
    1 lemon
    2 pints cream

Whisk all the ingredients together for half an hour and pour into a muslin-lined hair sieve to drain. Serve with hot baked marmalade pudding.

Marmalade Sponge

    4 oz (100 grammes) butter
    4 oz (100 grammes) sugar
    2 eggs, lightly beaten
    4 oz (100 grammes) flour
    ½ teaspoon baking powder
    1 tablespoon marmalade

Cream the butter and the sugar until light and fluffy. Stir in the eggs, and the flour and baking powder sifted together. Brush a pudding basin with melted lard, and in the base put a tablespoon or marmalade. Add the mixture, and bake in a moderately hot oven (350°F, Gas 4) for 1¼ hours.

Saint Columba's Cream

    8 oz cream cheese
    2 oz castor sugar
    2 fluid oz single cream

1 egg yolk
vanilla
brambles or blackcurrants to decorate

Blend all the ingredients except the fruit in a liquidiser and pour into individual glasses. Chill before serving. Top each with some berries. Serve with sponge fingers.

Sponge fingers

2 eggs, separated
2 oz sugar
2 oz plain flour

Beat the egg yolks and sugar until yellow and light. Stiffly beat the whites and sift the flour. Fold flour lightly into the mix and then the whites. Butter langue de chat tins and half fill with the mix. Bake in a moderately hot oven for 10 minutes or until browned. Cool.

Edinburgh Tart

6-8 oz (200 grammes) puff pastry
2 oz (50 grammes) butter
2 oz (50 grammes) sugar
2 oz (50 grammes) chopped candied peel
1 oz (25 grammes) sultanas
2 eggs, beaten

Roll out the puff pastry and use it to line an 8-inch pie plate or plain flan ring. Prick the bottom lightly. Melt the butter and the sugar in a small pan. Add the chopped candied peel, sultanas and the eggs. Pour into the pastry case and bake in a very hot oven (450°F, Gas 8). Serve hot or cold with a separate bowl of whipped cream.

Scotch Pudding

　　1 lb puff pastry
　　8 egg yolks
　　3 egg whites
　　8 oz castor sugar
　　4 oz melted butter
　　2 tablespoons ground rice
　　peel and juice of 1 lemon

Line a dish with the puff pastry. Mix all the rest of the ingredients and put into the pastry case. Bake in a moderate oven and turn it out to serve with castor sugar sifted over the top.

Cranachan

　　3-4 oz toasted sifted oatmeal
　　½ pint double cream
　　1 tablespoon rum
　　4-6 oz soft fruit (raspberries, brambles or blaeberries)

Toast the oatmeal in a frying pan until lightly browned. Sift off any dusty meal and then re-weigh the oatmeal. Half-whip the cream and add the rum. Fold in the meal and then the fruit. There should not be too much meal to cream. Serve in glasses.

Gaelic Coffee Jelly

2-3 oz icing sugar
½ oz gelatine
1 pint strong coffee
¼ pint whisky
1 oz castor sugar
½ pint double cream
1-2 tablespoons coffee sugar crystals

Dissolve the icing sugar and the gelatine in the coffee. When cool but not set stir in the whisky. Allow to set in a crystal serving bowl. Sweeten and whip the cream and spread thickly over the top of the jelly. Decorate with a border of dark coffee sugar crystals.

Cranberry Mousse

¼ oz gelatine
juice of 1 orange
½ pint sieved cranberry sauce
½ pint double cream
3 egg whites

Melt the gelatine very gently in the orange juice.

Continued on page 65

Opposite: Gingerbread (front) and Oatmeal Gingerbread
Next page: Easy Shortbread (left) Honey Shortbread (front) and Rich Shortbread

Add to the warmed sauce, then lightly fold in the half-whipped cream. Finally fold in the stiffly beaten egg whites. Turn into a soufflé dish to set and decorate with piped whipped cream.

Clootie Dumpling

6 oz margarine
3 cups flour
1 cup sugar
1 teaspoon baking soda
1 teaspoon cinnamon
1 teaspoon ginger
1 lb sultanas
½ lb currants
1 tablespoon treacle
1 tablespoon syrup
2 eggs, beaten
milk to mix

Rub margarine into the dry ingredients. Make a well and add the syrup, treacle and beaten egg and enough milk to make a stiff mix. Prepare a pudding cloth by dipping it into boiling water and then flour it generously. Put the mix on the cloth and tie well with string, allowing a good pocket for the pudding to expand. Boil for 3 hours.

Previous page: Scotch Black Bun
Opposite: A selection of Scottish Cheeses

Baking

Gingerbread

6 oz (200 grammes) butter
6 oz (200 grammes) soft brown sugar
6 oz (200 grammes) black treacle
1 lb (450 grammes) self-raising flour
2 teaspoons ginger
1 teaspoon baking soda dissolved in little water
2 knobs stem ginger, washed and chopped
milk

Grease and line a 10-inch square cake tin. Cream the butter, sugar and treacle. Sift the flour and ginger and stir into the treacle mix along with baking soda and water mix and chopped ginger knobs. Add enough milk to make a soft dropping consistency. Pour this batter into the prepared tin. Bake at 350°F (Gas 4-5) for 1½ hours or until firm to the touch. Cool on a wire tray and cut in squares to serve.

Dundee Cake

6 oz (170 grammes) butter
6 oz (170 grammes) castor sugar
3 eggs
9 oz (250 grammes) flour
½ teaspoon baking powder
6 oz (170 grammes) sultanas
3 oz (100 grammes) currants
3 oz (100 grammes) raisins
3 oz (100 grammes) mixed peel
1 oz (20 grammes) ground almonds
3 oz (100 grammes) blanched almonds
milk to mix

Cream the fat and sugar. Add the eggs one at a time and beat well. Add the dry ingredients, prepared fruit, and all but 1 oz of the blanched almonds. Add milk if necessary to make dropping consistency. Put in a greased and lined tin and place the rest of the almonds on top to make a pattern. Bake at 350°F (Gas 4) for 1½ hours. If not cooked lower heat to 300°F (Gas 2).

Illustrated overleaf

Parkins

8 oz (250 grammes) plain flour
8 oz (250 grammes) oatmeal
6 oz (170 grammes) sugar
¼ teaspoon baking soda
1 teaspoon ginger
1 teaspoon mixed spice
½ teaspoon cinnamon
4 oz (120 grammes) lard
1 egg
6 tablespoons syrup
almonds, halved

Mix all the dry ingredients. Rub in the lard. Put the egg and syrup in a bowl and whisk. Mix with the dry ingredients and roll into small balls. Put half an almond on each and slightly flatten. Bake for 15-20 minutes in a moderately hot oven (350°F, Gas 4). Cool on a wire rack.

Treacle Scones

8 oz (200 grammes) plain flour
½ teaspoon bicarbonate of soda
½ teaspoon cream of tartar
½ oz (15 grammes) castor sugar
½ teaspoon cinnamon
½ teaspoon mixed spice
pinch salt
2 oz (50 grammes) butter
2 tablespoons black treacle
4 fluid oz milk

Mix dry ingredients and rub in the fat. Mix the treacle and the milk together in a jug, and pour into a well in the middle of the dry ingredients. Mix with a broad-bladed knife to a dough. Knead lightly and roll out to about a quarter of an inch in thickness. Cut into 1½-inch rounds and brush with milk. Cook on a baking sheet at 400°F (Gas 6) for 10 minutes or until cooked. Makes 12. These scones keep very well.

Oatmeal Gingerbread

6 oz (200 grammes) lard
1 lb (500 grammes) plain flour
8 oz (250 grammes) fine oatmeal
6 oz (200 grammes) brown sugar
2 oz (50 grammes) stem ginger
2 teaspoons ground ginger
1 lb (500 grammes) golden syrup and treacle
  mixed

> 1 teaspoon bicarbonate of soda in 1 teacup of
>   warm milk
> 1 egg, beaten

Rub in the lard to the dry ingredients. Warm the syrup and treacle together until they run but are not hot. Add this mix to the dry ingredients. Add the milk and the egg. Pour into a lined and greased 9-inch (26-cm) tin and bake in a moderate oven (350°F, Gas 4) for 1-1¼ hours.

Seed Cake

> 6 oz (150 grammes) self-raising flour
> 1 teaspoon baking powder
> 1 teaspoon carraway seeds
> 4 oz (100 grammes) butter
> 4 oz (100 grammes) sugar
> 2 eggs
> 1 teaspoon whisky

Mix dry ingredients. Cream butter and sugar. Beat eggs and whisky together. Add with flour mixture to the creamed mix. Pour into a greased and base-lined 8-inch cake tin. Bake for 45 minutes at 350°F (Gas 4).

Drop Scones

8 oz (225 grammes) flour
½ teaspoon bicarbonate of soda
1 teaspoon cream of tartar
1 tablespoon sugar
1 egg
scant ½ pint (280 ml) milk

Sift the dry ingredients into a bowl. Drop the egg in the middle and add a little of the milk. Mix with a wooden spoon and beat until smooth. Gradually beat in enough milk to make the mix the consistency of thick cream. Butter a girdle well and have it hot (a thick-based frying pan will do if a girdle is unavailable). Drop the mix by tablespoons onto the girdle. When the bubbles rise and pop, turn them at once to cook on the other side. When nicely brown, put to cool wrapped in a tea towel on a cake cooling rack.

Easy Shortbread

6 oz (200 grammes) plain flour
6 oz (200 grammes) self-raising flour
3 oz (100 grammes) ground rice
2 oz (50 grammes) sugar
8 oz (300 grammes) butter

Mix all the dry ingredients. Melt the butter over a gentle heat and pour into the dry mix. Blend well with not too much handling. Pack into two 8-

inch (24 cm) sandwich tins. Smooth down and mark edges with a fork handle. Prick the centre well. Mark in 8 sections with a knife. Bake at 325°F (Gas 4) for 45 minutes. Sprinkle with sugar when hot, and cool in the tin.

Honey Shortbread

8 oz (200 grammes) self-raising flour
4 oz (100 grammes) butter
6 oz (150 grammes) honey
little milk

Work the flour, honey and butter together and then add just enough milk to make a stiff dough. Too much will make it tough. Roll out the dough and cut into shapes. Bake in a hot oven (375°F, Gas 5) until they are golden brown.

Shortbread

8 oz (200 grammes) butter
6 oz (150 grammes) self-raising flour
6 oz (150 grammes) plain flour
3 oz (75 grammes) ground rice
2 oz (50 grammes) sugar

Sift dry ingredients and rub in the butter. Knead to form a dough. Form into two rounds. Pack down well and smooth the tops. Mark edges and prick well. Bake at 350°F (Gas 4) for 45 minutes.

Rich Shortbread

1 oz (25 grammes) candied peel
1 oz (25 grammes) blanched almonds
8 oz (200 grammes) flour
1 oz (25 grammes) castor sugar
4 oz (100 grammes) butter

Cut the fruit and nuts into very small pieces. Mix with the flour and the sugar. Melt the butter and when it is cool pour onto the flour mixture, mixing it quickly. Form into four rounds about 1 inch thick, and pinch the edges with forefinger and thumb. Prick with a fork and put onto baking sheet lined with non-stick paper. Bake in a moderate oven (325°F, Gas 3) until lightly browned — about 1 hour.

Islay Loaf

1 cup raisins
1 cup currants
1 cup sugar
1 cup water
2 oz (50 grammes) butter
1 teaspoon bicarbonate of soda
2 cups self-raising flour
2 eggs, beaten

Into a pan put the fruits, sugar, water, butter, and bicarbonate of soda. Simmer gently for 15 minutes. Cool for a little while and then add the flour and the eggs. Pour the mixture into two 1 lb loaf tins, greased and lined. Bake for 1 hour at 350°F (Gas 5). Rest a few minutes when it comes from the oven and then turn out and cool on a wire tray.

Aberdeen Crulla

2 oz butter
2 oz castor sugar
2 beaten eggs
10 oz plain flour
oil for frying

Cream the butter and sugar. Add the eggs and then the flour, to form a soft dough. Roll out and cut into 5-inch by ½-inch strips and plait them. Fry these in deep hot oil until golden brown. Serve hot with sugar sprinkled over them.

Oatcakes

1 cup oatmeal
pinch bicarbonate of soda
¼ teaspoon salt
1 teaspoon melted lard
hot water to mix

Mix the dry ingredients. Add the fat and water to make a stiff dough. Roll out thinly on a board well-covered with dry meal. Cut into shapes. Heat a girdle or a thick frying pan and cook one side of the oatcakes until they curl. Toast the top under the grill to finish. Alternatively, the oatcakes may be baked in a moderately hot oven (375°F, Gas 5) until nicely cooked and dry.

Berwickshire Bombs

1 packet digestive biscuits
6 tablespoons hard margarine
1 small tin of condensed milk
3 tablespoons drinking chocolate
marshmallows
coconut and chocolate vermicelli

Crush the biscuits between two layers of grease-proof paper. Melt the margarine and milk in a pan and add the chocolate powder. Add the biscuits and mix well. Spread out on a plate to cool enough so it can be handled easily. Wrap a piece of this mixture round each marshmallow

76

making ball shapes. Roll half in chocolate vermicelli and half in coconut. Set in paper cases to
cool.

Forfar Fruit Loaf

4 oz (100 grammes) butter
4 oz (100 grammes) castor sugar
1 egg
8 oz (200 grammes) plain flour
1 teaspoon baking powder
1 tablespoon milk
4 oz (100 grammes) sultanas
4 oz (100 grammes) currants
1 oz (25 grammes) chopped almonds

Grease and line a 1 lb loaf tin. Cream the butter
and sugar. Add the eggs and flour alternately and
the baking powder with the last of the flour. Add
the milk. Stir in the fruits and the almonds. Mix
well and put into the prepared tin. Bake at 350°F
(Gas 4-5) for 1½-2 hours. Cool on a wire rack. Best
eaten the same day.

Ginger Iced Shortcake

8 oz (200 grammes) butter
4 oz (100 grammes) castor sugar
10 oz (250 grammes) plain flour
2 level teaspoons ginger
2 teaspoons baking powder

Icing

8 tablespoons icing sugar
4 oz (100 grammes) butter
5 tablespoons syrup
1½ teaspoons ginger

Cream the butter and sugar and fork in the flour, ginger and baking powder sifted together. Put in a greased square tin and bake at 325°F (Gas 3) for 40 minutes. Melt all the icing ingredients in a small pan and when thoroughly blended pour onto the hot shortcake. Cool and cut into squares.

Scotch Black Bun

12 oz flour and 6 oz fat made into a paste
1½ lb raisins
½ lb currants
2 oz blanched almonds, chopped
4 oz candied peel
8 oz flour
2 oz brown sugar
1 teaspoon cinnamon
1 teaspoon ginger
½ teaspoon nutmeg
¼ teaspoon black pepper
pinch cloves
½ teaspoon baking soda
3 eggs
2 tablespoons milk
1 tablespoon rum

Line a 9-inch tin with threequarters of the paste. In one bowl, mix all the dry ingredients, and in another bowl, whisk the eggs and milk with the rum. Add this to the dry ingredients and mix well. Push into the tin and put the lid of the remaining pastry on the top. Pierce right through several times with a skewer. Brush top with beaten egg and cook at 300°F (Gas 2) for 3 hours.

Aberdeen Butteries

3 oz (75 grammes) butter
8 oz (200 grammes) strong flour
½ teaspoon salt
1 teaspoon sugar
1 gill (140 ml) tepid water
1 teaspoon dried yeast
1 oz (25 grammes) lard

Rub 1 oz butter into the flour and salt. Melt sugar in water, add yeast. Stir until it dissolves. Pour into the flour and make a smooth dough. Knead well. Cover and leave to prove for 1 hour. Mix rest of butter and lard. Knead dough on a floured surface. Roll thin, spread on half of the fat, dust lightly with flour and fold in three. Seal the ends, quarter turn and roll again. Repeat fat spreading, dusting and folding. Cut into 12 squares, bring corners to the centre and knead into rounds. Dust a warm baking tray with flour. Leave to prove again for 30 minutes. Bake at 400°F (Gas 6) until pale gold.

Opposite: Swiss Milk Fudge (front) and Cinnamon Tablet

Caddiston Cake

14 oz (425 grammes) butter
1 lb (½ kilo) castor sugar
10 eggs
½ pint (280 ml) milk
6 fluid oz (12 tablespoons) golden syrup
2 lb (1 kilo) plain flour
2 teaspoons baking powder
1 lb (½ kilo) raisins
1 lb (½ kilo) currants
8 oz (200 grammes) mixed peel

Cream the butter and the sugar until very light.
Add the eggs one at a time. Heat the milk and the
syrup together and add them to creamed mix. Stir
in the flour and the baking powder and finally
add the fruits. Put in two 8-inch lined and greased
loose bottomed cake tins. Bake in a moderate
oven (325°F, Gas 3) for 3 hours or until a skewer
inserted in the middle comes out clean. This cake
keeps well.

Opposite: A selection of Preserves

Scones

8 oz (225 grammes) plain flour
1 teaspoon cream of tartar
½ teaspoon bicarbonate of soda
1 tablespoon sugar
pinch salt
2½ oz (60 grammes) butter
milk

Mix the dry ingredients and rub in the butter. Add some milk and mix to a stiff dough. Roll out on a floured board until it is about half an inch thick. Cut with a cutter and put on a floured baking sheet. Bake in a very hot oven (450°F, Gas 7) for 8-10 minutes.

Girdle Scones

8 oz (200 grammes) self-raising flour
salt
2 oz (50 grammes) butter
1 gill (140 ml) milk

Mix flour and salt. Rub in the butter and make into a soft dough with the milk. Knead lightly on a floured board and pat into a ½-inch thick round. Cut in wedges. Place on a preheated floured girdle and cook for 7-8 minutes. Turn gently with a spatula and do the other side until firm and cooked through.

Soda Scones

2 cups plain flour
½ teaspoon salt
2 teaspoons cream of tartar
1 teaspoon baking soda
1½ oz (40 grammes) butter
buttermilk to mix

Sift the dry ingredients together in a bowl and rub in the butter. Mix to a firm dough with a little buttermilk. Knead in the bowl for several minutes. Divide into small pieces and form into rounds. Prick with a fork and place on a baking sheet. Bake in a moderate oven (350°F, Gas 4-5) for 20 minutes.

Potato Scones

8 oz (200 grammes) mashed potato
½ oz (10 grammes) butter
pinch salt
2 oz (50 grammes) flour

Mash the potatoes or put through a potato ricer for a smooth texture. Add the butter and salt and beat well. Work in the flour by hand, and then roll out very thinly on a well-floured board. Cut into large rounds and then into quarters. Cook these on a hot girdle for about five minutes, turning when browned. Eat at once with butter for the best results.

A Mixture of Recipes

Scottish Cheeses

Scottish Cheddar
Both red and white versions are available and are made on a very large scale. They are on the whole pleasantly flavoured and excellent for cooking or for the cheese board.

Islay Dunlop
The Dunlop Cheeses are also produced either red or white, and are similar in many ways to a Cheddar. The Dunlop, however, is a slightly softer cheese and has a mellow flavour. This cheese makes excellent eating and may be used for cooking.

Orkney Cheese
The Orkney cheese started out as a farmhouse recipe, and had such a success that it is now a thriving industry. The cheese is produced red, white or smoked, which is a very pleasant cheese indeed. Serve as cheese on its own or in salads.

Stewart Cheeses

There are two Stewart cheeses, one blue and one white. The blue is reminiscent of Stilton, but lacks the distinctive character and flavour of that cheese. It is a milder cheese as well, and might be nice in a blue cheese salad dressing. The white Stewart is a rather salty cheese with very little character.

Crowdie

This is a cheese more often made in homes and cottages from the milk fresh from the cow, but is now a commercial cheese too. It is a soft cheese and comes in cartons. It can be good for salads or with bannocks. There is a version on the market in which it is blended with cream, making it very soft indeed.

Caboc

Caboc is a distinctive cheese made with cream and formed into cork shapes which are then rolled in oatmeal. Nice with oatcakes and a spot of black pepper.

There is a fluctuating number of other cheeses produced in Scotland. Some of these are more readily available in England than they are in their home country. One of these is Hramsa, which is a rich cream cheese flavoured with wild garlic. It is pleasant for a dip, but is not a good keeping cheese. There are also various cheeses that imitate none too well some of the French and Italian cheeses, and of course there is also a thriving industry producing good commercial cream and cottage cheeses, suitable for salads and for making cheese cakes.

Rhubarb Chutney

> 4 lb rhubarb
> 1 lb onions
> 1 lb sultanas
> ½ oz salt
> ½ oz ground ginger
> 2 oz mixed spice
> 1 lb soft brown sugar
> 1½ pints white vinegar

Prepare and cut up the rhubarb. Mince the onions and sultanas. Add the ginger, salt, mixed spice, white vinegar and sugar. Cook all together slowly until the rhubarb is tender. Continue cooking until the chutney is thick. Have some heated and sterilised jars ready and fill with the chutney using a jam funnel. Cover and store.

Jelly Marmalade

> 7 lb Seville oranges
> preserving sugar

Wash and dry the fruit. Using a zester take off all the rind. Take off the rest of the skin and pith. Cut up the fruit roughly. To each pound of prepared fruit allow 1 pint of water. Put fruit in water to soak for 24 hours. Boil gently until soft and strain through a jelly bag without using any pressure. Measure the juice and to each pint of liquid allow 1lb sugar. Mix the sugar, rind and juice together. Bring slowly to the boil. Boil fast until it jells when tested on a cold saucer. Skim thoroughly. Let the marmalade cool, stirring occasionally, before potting.

Grapefruit Marmalade

2½ lb grapefruit
4½ pints water
5½ lb sugar

Quarter the fruit and reserve the white pithy bits and the pips. Slice the fruit thinly in a dish so as not to lose the juice. Take some of the measured water and put with the pips and pith. Add the rest of the water to the fruit and allow to stand for 24 hours. Strain the liquid from the pips into the rest of the fruit and put to boil. Boil for 1 hour and then add the sugar and boil for another hour. Put into clean and warm pots using a jam funnel.

Rusty Nail

1 measure of malt whisky
1 measure of Drambuie

Mix together and serve as an after dinner liqueur. This is indeed the nail in the coffin . . . *Serves 1.*

Crowdie

   1 pint fresh milk
   ¼ teaspoon rennet
   salt

Warm the milk to blood heat very gently. If possible use a thermometer and keep it at 72°F. Add the rennet and stir in. Set in a dish to cool and when the whey rises cut the curd into squares. Pour into a hair sieve or a muslin cloth. Allow to drip until all the whey is gone — about two hours, or overnight if you have time. Break up the curd with a fork, and squeeze gently. Season with salt to taste and put into a jar or bowl in the fridge. Use within 48 hours.

Note: Pasteurised milk may be used but the cheese will have less flavour and will not keep so well. Allowing the milk to overheat will make the cheese tough.

Grapefruit Chutney

   4 grapefruit
   1 lb firm onions
   1½ oz salt
   1 pint white vinegar
   1½ teaspoons ground ginger
   4 oz raisins
   1½ lb demerara sugar
   ¼ teaspoon pepper
   ½ teaspoon dry mustard

Wipe the fruit and slice thinly. Remove the pips. Chop the onions finely and put in a dish. Sprinkle with the salt and leave to stand for 24 hours. Put in a pan and add the rest of the ingredients. Bring slowly to the boil and simmer for one hour. Have some sterilised pots standing by and fill through a jam funnel. Cover when quite cold.

Ayrshire Potatoes and Cream Cheese

10 even sized new Ayrshire potatoes
3-4 oz cream cheese
1 tablespoon milk
black pepper
salt
chopped parsley, mint and tarragon
snipped chives to taste

Scrub the potatoes and boil them in salted water until tender but not overcooked. Drain and dry off, then allow the potatoes to cool a little but not to chill. Slacken the cream cheese with the milk, adding a little more if needed. Season with salt and pepper and add the herbs. With a melon scoop or a teaspoon, scoop a round out of each potato. Fill the cavities with the cheese filling and top each with a sprig of parsley. The potatoes may then be eaten warm in the fingers.

Swiss Milk Fudge

    4 oz butter
    1 cup milk
    2 lb sugar
    1 large tin condensed milk
    2 teaspoons vanilla

Put the butter and the milk in a copper or thick-based pan and melt gently. Add the sugar and allow to dissolve completely. Bring to the boil, and boil for 10 minutes. Add the tin of condensed milk and the vanilla. Stir, and bring back to the boil. Boil for another ten minutes. Beat hard for 1-2 minutes and then pour the fudge into a buttered Swiss roll tin. Mark in squares before it is set otherwise it will not break cleanly.

A Brew of Hot Ale

    1 lemon
    2-inch piece cucumber
    ½ pint red wine
    ¼ pint dry cider
    2-3 oz sugar lumps
    2-inch stick cinnamon
    2-3 cloves
    blade of mace
    1 orange
    1 apple
    few grapes

Remove strips of rind from the lemon and cucumber. Slice thinly and reserve good slices for serving. Put the wine and cider into a pan with the sugar. Heat slowly until the sugar is dissolved. Add the trimmings of the lemon and cucumber, the spices and 2-3 slices of orange and apple. Bring slowly to simmering point, or until the surface is covered with white foam. Remove from the heat. Have apple rings, orange slices, cucumber and lemon slices and a few grapes in a warm jug. Strain in the mulled wine and serve in warm glasses with frosted edges or decorate with a twist of orange or lemon.

Brose

1 handful oatmeal per person
salt

Mix the salt and oats in a basin. Pour on enough boiling water to wet well but not to have it swimming. Stir and stand for a few minutes to let the meal swell, keeping it hot. Serve with cream.

Oatmeal Fritters

> 2 tablespoons oatmeal
> 1 tablespoon flour
> ½ teaspoon baking powder
> pinch salt
> 2-3 fluid oz milk
> goose fat, or bacon fat

Mix the dry ingredients and add enough milk to make a moderately fluid batter. Heat the goose fat, or bacon fat and drop the mix by spoonfuls into it. Fry until brown and set and turn over to do the other side. Delicious served with bacon and eggs.

Cinnamon Tablet

> 2 lb sugar
> 2 teacups milk
> 4 oz butter
> 1 oz powdered cinnamon

Boil the sugar, milk and butter in a thick pan very gently for 35 minutes. Remove from the heat. Mix the cinnamon with a little water and add it to the sugar mixture. Beat hard until sugar begins to harden on the sides of the pan. Pour into buttered plates or tins to set. Mark into pieces while still warm.

Fudge

1 lb brown sugar
1 gill water
2 oz butter

Dissolve the sugar in the water and add the butter. Boil together until 240°F is reached on a sugar thermometer or until a soft ball forms when tested in cold water. Pour into greased trays and cut as it cools.

Orange Marmalade

2 lb Seville oranges
2 lemons
8 lb preserving sugar
1 sweet orange

Cut the fruit into quarters. Remove the pips and put them into a bowl. Slice the fruit on a plate so as not to lose the juices. Take a measured four pints of water and put some on the pips and the rest in with the fruit. Stand like this for 24 hours. Strain the pips and add this liquid to the rest. Put in a large preserving pan and boil for 2 hours until tender. Warm the sugar slightly. Add the sugar and boil for a further hour or until the marmalade is setting when tested on a cold saucer. Pot, using a jam funnel, and cover when cold.

Index